I Want to Be a Police Officer

Written by Peter J

This book belongs to

_____

When I grow up, I want to be a police officer. Police officers help keep people safe and stop bad guys from doing illegal things.

Police officers get to drive around in cool police cars with flashing lights and loud sirens. When there is an emergency, they rush to help people right away!

Police officers have to wear special uniforms too. They wear dark blue shirts and pants with badges on them. They also wear belts to hold things like handcuffs, flashlights, gun, and radios.

To be a police officer, you have to be very brave. Police officers sometimes have to chase bad guys and arrest them! They aren't scared to face danger to protect people.

Police officers also have to be very fit and strong. They train hard to stay in good shape. They exercise a lot and practice defense moves like tackling or punching.

Being a police officer means helping people in the community every day. They give directions when someone is lost, rescue kittens from trees, and keep neighborhoods safe.

Police officers have to be good listeners too. When there is an accident or crime, they interview witnesses to figure out what happened. Listening carefully helps them solve mysteries!

They also need to know all the traffic and safety laws. There is a lot of studying at the police academy to become an officer! You have to pass some very hard tests.

Police officers work during the day and night. They take turns working different shifts to patrol around the clock. Late at night can be very busy with more emergencies happening.

Police officers have an important job keeping the peace. They risk their lives every day. We should thank them for their bravery and service in protecting us.

When I see a police car go by with its siren on, I feel proud. I know they are racing off to make our community safer. I want to grow up to be as helpful as them!

I know being a police officer can be dangerous, but I won't be scared. I will get strong to face any bad guy and rescue people in need. Nothing will stop me from helping others!

I hope I can be as smart, brave, and helpful as a police officer when I grow up. I want to stop crimes and make sure everyone follows the rules. No one will get away with doing illegal things in my town!

One day, I'll go to the police academy for training. I will study hard to know all the laws and be in top shape physically. Then I'll get to put on my official uniform for the first time!

When I finally become a police officer, I'll be so proud. I'll get my badge, handcuffs, radio, and gun. Then I'll go out on patrol in my police car, ready to serve and protect my community!

Being a police officer takes courage and a willingness to face danger. But I'm not afraid – I can't wait to say "Officer reporting for duty!" when I grow up. This is what I was meant to do!

Peter J wholeheartedly cheers on every child with dreams, urging them to follow their passions, and sincerely hopes that their dreams come true. If you enjoy Peter J's book, we would truly appreciate your feedback in the form of a review and a star rating. Your thoughts and ratings mean a lot, as Peter J is committed to creating even more enjoyable books for your reading delight. Thank you wholeheartedly for your ongoing support.

By the same author: Peter J
Already published:

Made in the USA
Las Vegas, NV
08 October 2024

96426180R00024